11 Secrets to MANAGE PROJECTS and REMAIN STRESS-FREE

SUSHIL GUPTA

PG PUBLICATION
Delhi - 110089 (India)

Edition : 2024
ISBN : 978-81-969041-0-4

Price : 400/-

11 Secrets to Manage Projects and Remain Stress-Free
By : Sushil Gupta

Cover Page & Layout
Jyoti Singh

Published by

PRAKHAR GOONJ PUBLICATION
Reg. Office: H-3/2 Sector-18 Rohini, Delhi-110089
Office : A-4/57 Sector-18 Rohini, Delhi-110089
Email : prakhargoonj@gmail.com
info@prakhargoonjpublications.com
Ph. : 7982710571, 7838505899, 011-42635077
Web : prakhargoonjpublications.com

About the Author

The Author is a Project Manager by profession, working for a multinational company for the execution of a project of about 4500 crores. He has experience of almost 30 years in the construction industry. He has experience in managing various projects in Dubai, Abu Dhabi and Bahrain apart from India for various projects like Marine work, power plants, buildings, and infrastructures.

He has worked on various projects as a project manager with Contracting firms, Consultants and Clients as well. He is a qualified Civil Engineer with an MBA and various project management certifications like PMP- PMI (USA) and NICMAR- Pune.

The Author wants to convey the approach to be adopted in the workplace and our lives, whether we are working Professionals, Entrepreneurs, Students, or aspirant Managers, through which one can solve their problems and maintain happiness in life. The Author has been practicing Rajyoga Meditation for 11 years and is associated with Prajapita Brahmakumaries Ishwariya Vishwavidyalaya. The Author wants to bust the myth that stress or tension is the outcome of work pressure and stiff professional targets and explains how it is due to our bad habits and irregular lifestyles.

FOREWORD

In the fast-paced world of project management, where demands are high, and timelines are often tighter than we'd like, the pursuit of effective and stress-free project delivery seems like an elusive goal. The Author Sushil Gupta, experienced in the intricate realm of project management, masterfully unveils the hidden gems that can transform chaos into calmness and stress into serenity.

In "11 Secrets to Manage Projects and Remain Stress-Free," the Author Sushil Gupta takes us on a journey beyond conventional methodologies. This is not just another project management manual; it is a compass for navigating the challenges with finesse and maintaining one's sanity in the process. As we delve into the pages of this book, we are invited to uncover the secrets that lie at the intersection of practicality and peace of mind.

What makes this book truly exceptional is the Author Sushil Gupta's ability to distil years of experience into eleven actionable secrets. These are not merely abstract concepts but tangible, real-world strategies that project managers can apply at any stage of their careers. From fostering effective communication to mastering the art of prioritization, each secret is a stepping stone toward a more organized, efficient, and stress-free project management experience.

As you embark on this journey, be prepared to be enlightened, challenged, and inspired. The secrets within these pages are not just tools; they are keys to unlocking a new paradigm of project management—one where success is measured not only in deliverables but also in the peace of mind of those orchestrating the projects.

In a world that thrives on complexity, The book reminds us that simplicity and clarity are the cornerstones of effective project management. This book is a testament to the fact that managing projects need not be synonymous with stress; it can be a fulfilling and rewarding endeavour.

As you embark on this journey through the Art of Stress-Free Living, be prepared to be gently guided into a realm where mindfulness, self-care, and intentional living become not just concepts but cherished companions on your path to tranquillity. Each chapter unfolds like a treasure trove, offering practical exercises, thought-provoking reflections, and a roadmap to navigate the complexities of our inner landscapes.

May this book be your trusted companion on the path to stress-free project management, offering insights, strategies, and a refreshing perspective that transforms the way you approach and lead projects.

Sister BK USHA
Management Trainer,
Motivational Speaker
Senior Teacher in Brahma Kumaris
Mt. Abu- Rajasthan

DEDICATION

I am grateful to my Supreme Godfather, my mortal body father, my mother, friends, colleagues and my seniors, whose well-wishes, encouragement, and support were crucial in completing this assignment. I express my gratitude to everyone whose support made this publication possible.

My special thanks to sister BK Anu (Rajula- India), sister BK Anusuya (Bahrain), and sister BK Bharti (Abu Dhabi), whose teachings, support and guidance helped me to overcome many situations in life.

Above all, I owe a debt of gratitude to my wife, Kanchan Gupta, and my sons, Utkarsh and Ujval, who inspired and helped me to maintain my concentration long enough to finish this book on schedule.

Additionally, to all the individuals and young people worldwide who, upon discovering their own limitless potential, may reach the pinnacle of affluence and fulfill all of them.

Also, to all people and young people around the world who can create a Blissful society by realizing the infinite power within oneself, one can reach the pinnacle of ultimate prosperity, realize all dreams and desires, change the scenario of the whole world, and create a complete, healthy and prosperous society.

We have taken enough from the universe, and now it's time to return.

Summary of Book

- Are you tired of working under stress on a project,
- Not able to achieve targets,
- Struggling with team performance,
- Want to improve productivity, not happy with your organization or team,
- Want to develop a team with leadership skills, management skills, and mind management?

if yes, this book is for you, specifically for Entrepreneurs, Managers, and Students.

The Book "11 Secrets to Manage Projects and Remain Stress-Free" describes the approaches and techniques to be adopted for personnel transformation, developing inner strength, increasing productivity, and effective management by being more organized, more focused, and working smarter.

In today's world, organizations are seeking adaptable, profitable, and productive approaches to reach their objectives, and successful project management is the solution. Project management is not only a highly sought-after skill in almost every sector, but it is also among the most flexible skills that you can acquire.

Whether you're someone who is hesitant to take on the role of a project manager, a manager who has recently been assigned project responsibilities, or a business owner seeking to expand your business, it is possible to acquire and apply top-notch project management expertise to accomplish your objectives.

What you learn here.

- Creating a Healthier working environment.
- Completing all work on time and enjoying life.
- Positive mindset.
- Better relationship.

- Self-discipline- to turn your dreams into reality.
- Positive thinking and affirmation.
- How to recharge your mind.
- Increase inner power.
- Effective management.

This self-improvement book is one of the most promising things that you can gift to yourself or your loved ones. One can get the best out of oneself. The author believes that people possess a wealth of knowledge but lack the necessary tools to implement it effectively. That is the reason why the Author tried to keep this book very simple and did not mention complicated steps or procedures. so that readers get some value from this book. This book is very simple even if you don't need to refer to a dictionary.

Bose- "Can't you get any closer?"
Captain- "Am afraid not, sir, we could collide."
Bose- "What do you suggest?"
Captain- "I recommend that- you go back."
Bose, looking at the 20 feet high waves
"Captain, I haven't come
all this way just to go back!"

- Once you reach the high point using a ladder, then throw the ladder,
- Once you cross a valley using the bridge, then cut the bridge.
- Once you reach the land using a boat, then drown the boat.

It is said for the Military. So that you can't go back once you have chosen a path. Take it with confidence.

How To Read This Book

1. There are no guidelines for reading this book, so go ahead and read it in any capacity or request you need.
2. Avoid the parts that are not important to you. No, you don't need to peruse a book cover to cover.
3. Feature text and take notes to recall more.
4. Skimming a book before you read it very well may be helpful. I frequently skim a book so I can get a superior comprehension of what I ought to skip or zero in on. Occasionally, I can't miss anything.
5. You only need one idea that can change your life. If a book gives you only one good piece of advice, it's already worth your time.

HAPPY READING

Content

INTRODUCTION

Gratitude fills my heart as I receive this award for my contributions to various projects from one of India's influential organizations. In this moment of recognition, "I would like to dedicate this honor to my father, who is present in this hall. I request all of you to join me in acknowledging his presence with a resounding round of applause."

Post the award ceremony, a conference proceeded, exploring the journey that led me to this point. The interviewer extended congratulations and expressed curiosity about my path to becoming a Project Manager. Recognizing the uniqueness I bring to life, the conversation touched upon the inspiration and footsteps that others may follow.

The audience was informed of my commitment to society through valuable contributions such as team building, motivational speeches, corporate training, and workshops addressing child behaviour by the interviewer. The interviewer, having personally attended several of these sessions, conveyed joy and satisfaction at this moment.

Allow me to guide you through my journey from childhood to the present. Reflecting on my time in fifth grade. The interviewer inquired about my early arrival at the function. In response, I shared a lesson instilled by my father—punctuality.

Punctuality

Time, he emphasized, is a commitment that should be honored, a principle he lived by and imparted to me. Punctuality, in my father's philosophy, was more than a mere habit—it was a guiding principle that shaped not just the moments before a meeting but the entirety of one's approach to life.

He would often elaborate on the concept, emphasizing that punctuality is a sign of respect for others' time and a testament to one's reliability. It was a discipline that extended beyond professional settings, becoming a fundamental aspect of personal integrity.

In business, my father's punctuality wasn't just about being on time; it was a strategic move. Those crucial minutes before a meeting were dedicated to cultivating a positive mindset by radiating positive vibrations and setting the stage for success. As he sat in anticipation, he would immerse himself in thoughts that radiated positivity:

- I am powerful.
- I am going to succeed in my life.
- The person is very loving and will understand what I say.
- He is a lovely person.
- Thanks to God, life, and nature for helping me.
- This meeting will give the result that I am expecting.

These affirmations, born in those precious pre-meeting minutes, weren't merely words; they were a conscious effort to manifest a favorable environment filled with positive vibrations.

As a curious observer, I would often question my father about the practicality of this ritual. "Do you always find success by doing so?" I would ask. His response, delivered with a calm certainty, was, "Yes, most of the time." Yet, he maintained that the focus should not solely be on the outcome; instead, the emphasis lay on creating an atmosphere favorable to success.

In the larger tapestry of life, according to my father, punctuality wasn't just a virtue—it was a cornerstone of personal and professional integrity. This practice rippled through every facet of one's journey. As I carry this legacy forward, I find myself not merely adhering to a schedule but embracing a profound commitment to honor time—a commitment instilled in me by a father who understood the timeless value of punctuality.

We need to think positively, but the outcome also depends on many other external factors. You need not be thinking about the result.

Managing your workplace reputation is critical for success, and punctuality is crucial to building a positive professional image. Being consistently punctual offers several benefits:

1. **Reliability and Dependability:** Punctual employees are often perceived as reliable. Arriving on time and meeting deadlines consistently demonstrates your commitment to your work and team.
2. **Professionalism:** Punctuality is a hallmark of professionalism. It reflects a respect for others' time, a commitment to your responsibilities, and an understanding of the importance of deadlines in a professional setting.
3. **Consistency and Predictability:** Punctual individuals contribute to a more predictable and consistent work environment. Knowing that a colleague or team member is consistently on time fosters a sense of reliability and stability in the workplace.
4. **Positive Workplace Morale:** A punctual employee contributes to positive workplace morale. When team members can rely on each other to be on time, it enhances trust and collaboration.
5. **Reduce stress:** Punctuality helps manage stress for yourself and your colleagues. When everyone is on time and meets deadlines, it reduces the need for last-minute rushes, decreasing stress levels in the workplace.
6. **Professional Image:** Being punctual builds a positive professional image. It sends a message to colleagues, superiors, and clients that you are organized, responsible, and take your work seriously.
7. **Effective use of time:** Punctuality allows for

more efficient use. It helps plan and allocate time effectively, improving productivity and better outcomes for projects and tasks.

8. **Leadership Qualities:** Punctual individuals often exhibit leadership qualities. Being on time sets an example for others.
9. **Professional Relationship:** Punctuality contributes to positive professional relationships. Colleagues and superiors are likelier to trust and appreciate individuals who consistently meet their commitments and timelines.

CHAPTER: 1
NEVER SAY "NO"

Father: YES means "I can," and NO means "I can't."

Yes means "I believe in myself" and NO means "I doubt myself".

Yes means "Power," and NO means "Weakness."

Yes means "Passion" No means "Disinterest".

Remove the word "NO" from your dictionary same as the word Impossible was not in the dictionary of Napoleon.

Every human being has an inherent goodness that allows them to distinguish between good or bad, right, or wrong. However, they often lack the willpower to follow through with their own moral compass. Their mindset is similar to that of Duryodhana's. Today's society is filled with capable individuals, but many possess an ego that prevents them from accepting the word "NO". They crave universal acceptance and find it difficult to tolerate rejection.

Everyone possesses inherent strengths and weaknesses. It is crucial to identify the individual's strengths and empower them to overcome their weaknesses. Selecting the best person for a managerial role is a challenging task. Similarly, it can be tough for an employee to find a job that meets all their preferences. Therefore, we must work collaboratively to support each other in achieving our goals.

Why you should not say NO

Son: "What should I do if someone assigns me a task that I am unfamiliar with and do not know how to complete? Should I decline the task to save the other person's time and energy?"

Father: It's possible that you may not be aware of your own abilities, but it's likely that someone else recognizes them.

Son: How is it possible that I am not aware of my abilities?

Father: There could be two reasons for someone assigning you a task you've never done before.

One- He believes in you and your abilities because you are sincere and hard-working. You can achieve great things.

Second- He wants you to be capable of completing a task, so you must acquire the skills and knowledge necessary to do it. If you're faced with a task that you're not familiar with, you should gather all the relevant information, research the subject, and explore all possible options to complete it. Similarly, if you're given a task, you should view it as a challenge and find a way to complete it. Don't hesitate to ask for help from your colleagues, even those who are less experienced than you. The most important thing is to always be learning.

While learning you get to know new ideas and will have a good command of the subject matter. It will give you a sense of power, energy, and positive working culture within the team. You will be the example for everyone in your team and they will also learn the power of "YES". There should be a thirst for knowledge. If you don't get into a new and challenging job, you won't get a chance to develop yourself.

I can live my life as I choose, but is that the purpose of life? When I live my life with a clear focus and without confusion, stress, or anxiety, based on its true value, I experience a sense of fulfillment and purpose.

Son: Dad, what if someone intentionally gives me more tasks despite me already working hard?

Father: Well, it's a possibility. There could be various reasons behind it. Maybe they see your potential and believe you can handle more responsibilities. On the other hand, if you feel it's becoming excessive or affecting your current work, you should definitely address it.

Son: But why would someone do that?

Father: Managers usually have reasons for assigning tasks. It could be to challenge you, help you grow, or they might not be fully aware of your current workload. However, if you ever feel overwhelmed or that it's affecting your performance, it's crucial to communicate. Open and honest communication is key in the workplace.

Son: How do I approach that conversation?

Father: Be respectful and honest. Share your concerns about the workload and how it might impact your ability to deliver quality work. It could be that they are not aware of the extent of your tasks. And remember, it's not a sign of weakness to discuss workload; it shows responsibility and a commitment to delivering your best work.

Son: That makes sense. I'll try talking to them and see if we can find a solution.

Father: Good plan. Remember, effective communication is a skill that will serve you well in both your personal and professional life.

Benefit of Saying YES

Father: It is very easy for someone to say no if he doesn't want to do the task. The benefit of saying YES is:

- You will learn new skills.
- Demonstrated cooperation with others.
- People will like you.
- You demonstrate- can-do attitude.
- You feel good by being helpful.
- You will also get favour in the future.

Where to Say No

Son: let's assume someone called me for a party, and I don't want to go. Then what should I do?

Father: In that case, you can tell your friend clearly that you don't want to come due to some reason. If you say that you will try to come, and you already decided that you will not go. Then it's better to say him now. Generally, people don't dare to say no in this kind of situation because they don't have the power to listen to "NO".

The myth: Saying "yes" to too many demands is exhausting.

CHAPTER: 2

SET A POSSIBLE BUT DIFFICULT TARGET

Father: Do you know the difference between Goal and Target?

Son: It seems both are the same. The goal and target are the specific points that an individual or organization aims to reach or accomplish.

Father: There are major differences. Goals are made considering long-term vision, mentioning what a company is willing to achieve with deadlines. Targets are smaller than Goal. It is a series of steps toward achieving the goal. Targets are to be achieved by individuals and teams of any organization, and goals are to be achieved by the organization.

Target Setting

Son: How can I set a goal in my life?

Father: To lead a fulfilling life, it's crucial to have a clear vision of what you want to achieve in the future. To make that vision a reality, it's recommended to set measurable goals and break them down into smaller milestones. This approach enables you to track your progress and stay motivated along the way. So, take the time to identify your goals for the next few years and map out a plan to reach them. Remember, every step counts!

For example, A student is preparing for the Olympiad exams, which are national and international level exams offered by the Indian Talent Olympiad going to be held in 9 months. Now you need to be ready to appear in the exam. You need to prepare a study plan/ strategy. List out the books you need to study. References need to be made. Previous year's questions to be reviewed. Now the list of documents to be studied is ready with you. You need to assign the time required to study these books. You assign sometimes for revision and mock tests and then you start following your study plan. Also don't forget to monitor your plan. If you are behind your schedule, then you need to re-plan the activity, revise it, and again repeat the same process.

Son: How to set a target?

Father: If you want to achieve anything, you need to set a Target. Without a target, you can't achieve anything. Suppose you sent a target to complete reading your favorite book in 15 days and the book has 150 pages, then you need to set a target to complete the reading of at least 10 pages every day before going to bed. If you miss your target any day, then the next day, you double your target, say 20 pages, as a punishment. It is not punishment actually; it is good for your progress. Do you know how many books were read by President Bush? 95 books in a year.

It is important to hold yourself accountable in a way that will ultimately benefit you. Personally, I set a goal to read 42 books in a year, with an average completion time of 9 days per book. Although I did not successfully achieve this, I did complete almost half of my goal and read a total of 22 books in the year. I also remember setting a target to complete reading a full 300 pages of a book in one day, which I was able to accomplish. A target should not be easily achievable, otherwise it is not really a target. It should be set in such a way that it is quite difficult to achieve.

Suppose you want to learn how to play the guitar. You ask around and everyone tells you it takes at least a month to learn. However, you decide to challenge yourself and set a goal to learn in just 15 days. I would suggest keeping this goal to yourself and not sharing it with anyone. With determination and hard work, you can prove that it's possible to achieve this goal in just 15 days.

The target should be –

A. Quite impossible to achieve.

B. It should give a sense of motivation.

C. It is important not to prioritize your eating and sleeping habits over achieving your targets.

D. You should not waste time on useless thoughts that drain your energy.

E. It should be focused on activities that need

improvement, not those in which you are already proficient.

F. When you reach your goal, you feel a sense of accomplishment and joy, and your tiredness fades away. You feel refreshed, even after working hard to achieve your goal. You don't feel like taking a break because you feel motivated. This increased energy can improve your productivity and inspire you to work with greater enthusiasm and motivation.

A person does not become tired because of work alone. Rather, it is the lack of a clear target, interest, zeal, and enthusiasm that leads to exhaustion. It is important to love your work and workplace and to give your full effort to your tasks. Regardless of the type of work you are doing; it is essential to approach it with honesty and dedication. For instance, even a cleaner sweeping the floor should do so with a positive attitude, striving to create a unique and perfect result. By doing so, anyone who enters the room will appreciate the cleanliness and wonder about the person who takes care of the office or house.

I have an example of an area where I used to struggle, which was replying to emails promptly. Sometimes, it would take me two days to respond, and other times it would take me as long as four days. This was frustrating, and I knew I needed to improve. One day, I decided to set a goal for myself: to respond to all emails within 24 hours. I've been achieving this goal every day, and it has greatly improved my productivity. I feel much happier now, and most importantly, I save time. The key is to have determination and strong willpower when setting goals. In order to increase productivity, it's helpful to surround yourself with others who are also productive.

One more example of goal setting is when I set a target to resolve all the pending issues of all the departments that are one week old. By doing this, you won't have to waste time reviewing matters that are older than one week after resolving them. It will save time.

Son: How do you know nothing is pending?

Father: It is a good question. I will tell you later.
"The key to achieving the target is to work with a sense of urgency. You may have heard that every task should be planned in a way that eliminates urgency and allows for smooth completion. However, I disagree with this approach."

Son: Is it the only way to set the goal?
Father: Yes, setting goals is important because it helps you stay motivated and directs your attention towards what you need to do to achieve success. At times, you may feel like you have put in a lot of effort but achieved very little over the years. It can also be challenging to figure out how to accomplish your goals in the coming years.

To achieve your goals, it's important to stay focused and keep track of your progress, just like an army general who constantly monitors the map to check the area conquered by his army. He also keeps an eye on the weapons, ammunition, and equipment they have in stock, and how much they have advanced towards their future aim. The general observes the distance left to reach their destination and the speed at which they are advancing towards it.

Many individuals frequently switch jobs in search of success, often working less. If you want to achieve SMART goals, you need to have a clear understanding, focus on your work, utilize your time efficiently, and use resources wisely.

Son: All the examples you gave are for an organization. Can you give any examples to improve my relationship with my friends? So that I can guide them to set a target.

Father: It's not possible to force someone else to set a target in a relationship. The best thing to do is to set a target for yourself and work towards it. Improving a relationship is a journey, and it requires a long-term goal. One way to achieve this is to aim to avoid arguing with your partner on a daily basis. However, it's easy to forget this target when your friend says something that upsets you and you react impulsively. This can potentially ruin your relationship. It is crucial to be aware and focused on your objectives.

Son: How is the target to be achieved then? Is this an unachievable target?

Father: No, not all. It is the most difficult target because here ego takes precedence. You will think you are right at any point in time, and you will blame your friend for differences. In the same way, your friend also will be thinking. That is the reason, the relationship is not repaired and is damaged day by day.

Son: What is the solution then?

Father: When you bend your body downwards, you strengthen your muscles. Similarly, when you lower your ego, you strengthen your soul. You can try this technique as it is a master key to all the tips. Whenever you argue with your friend, express your opinion with a lovely smile and have good wishes for your friend. Make it your daily goal to achieve this. Success will come in your footsteps, but it's difficult to predict when. By following this, you will also increase your tolerance power.

What if Target is not Achieved

Son: What if I did not achieve the target?

Father: It is often said that it is okay to miss the target, but lowering your target is not a sign of success. It's important to review your target periodically and make necessary adjustments. This may include revising the target end date or increasing daily output. Once you achieve your target, it's time to set a new one with an increased output. For example, if your target was to run 5 km daily for a month, after achieving it, you should aim to run 6 km daily the next month, 7 km the following month, and so on.

Son: "If someone has a set of goals or targets, what should they do?"

Father: It is important to set priorities for goals and track progress using Key Performance Indicators (KPIs).

Son: Setting goals can be a challenging task, and I often feel exhausted from the process.

Father: As I mentioned earlier, feeling tired is not necessarily caused by work itself. If you love your work and workplace, you are less likely to experience fatigue. Instead, tiredness can result from carrying extra burdens such as wasted thoughts, unhealthy eating and sleeping habits, lack of exercise, and no motivation in life. However, if you are passionate about your goals, achieving them will become much easier.

"If you don't have your own goals, you'll be doomed to work toward someone else's." -Harry Truman

Your goals determine the qualifications you need and the symptoms you show. For example, if your goal is to become a doctor, you need to go to school to learn the skills and knowledge required for the job. These qualifications would include a medical degree, a license to practice medicine, and other certifications. The symptoms you would show as a doctor could include things like knowing how to diagnose illnesses, providing treatment, and giving advice to patients. It's important to identify your goals early on and work hard to acquire the necessary qualifications to achieve them. By doing so, you increase your chances of exhibiting favorable symptoms that align with your aspirations.

Leave Your Comfort Zone

Set goals that will ignite your passion, test your limits, and transform you into a better version of yourself.

Acknowledge the immense value of taking risks and stepping out of your comfort zone.

1. It is important to acknowledge that staying in "Your comfort zone may be hindering you from having new experiences" and personal growth.
2. Just remember that sometimes it's valuable to feel uncomfortable.
3. Lean in.

4. By taking up new challenges and stepping out of your comfort zone, you can significantly enhance your personal growth and foster a more fulfilling life experience.
5. This may require a change in mindset.
6. It would be helpful to acknowledge your fear.
7. Own the negative emotions that arise.
8. Decide if the rewards outweigh the fear.
9. "Try not to think too much about it."
10. Don't get caught up thinking too much or analysing everything, it can make you freeze up and not be able to make a decision.
11. Sometimes, you have to take the next step even when you're not sure what the end goal is.

Learning From Failure

After a few months-

Son: Dad, today was my 200 M running competition. Don't you want to know the result?

Father: Yes, of course. I want to know the result, but I am more interested in what you learn from the outcome. How do you see the result?

Son: After practicing for a long time, I was disappointed to lose the competition and come in third place. I'm wondering if there is any lesson I can learn from this experience.

Father: One should focus on learning from results, whether winning or losing, instead of wasting time on regret. The mind should immediately switch from problem to solution, always looking for solutions instead of problems.

You can learn a lot of things from failure such as:

a) You have experience of one failure.

b) Now you will try another way of attempting the situation.

c) You get the time for inner engineering.

You have the opportunity to develop the virtue of tolerance, which will help you build inner strength and resilience. This is a priceless attribute that cannot be purchased with money.

STORY: A manager made a mistake in the factory, resulting in losses for the company. The manager expressed regret and offered to resign, but the owner refused to accept the resignation. Instead, the owner asked the manager what he plans to do next. The manager replied that he will apply for a job in another company. The owner then asked if the manager intends to use the same method that led to the previous losses. The manager responded that it would be unwise to use the same method since it may lead to losses again. The manager expressed that he does not want to repeat the same mistake.

Then, the Owner said now you have gained the experience of failure. Why don't you do the same thing here, and where will I get a person who has the experience of one failure? The owner becomes a bestower (giver), then only he can do this. The owner emphasizes the importance of learning from mistakes and applying that experience to improve rather than repeating the same errors elsewhere. The owner takes on a mentoring role, encouraging the manager to use the gained experience as a stepping stone for growth and improvement.

This story underscores the idea that failure can be a powerful teacher, and individuals should learn from their mistakes to become better at their jobs and in life. The owner's perspective reflects a positive approach to handling setbacks, turning them into opportunities for personal and professional development.

"Take the opportunity to learn from your mistakes: find the cause of your problem and eliminate it. Don't try to be perfect; just be an excellent example of being human."

--Tony Robbins

Some people find SMART Goals very complicated. So, make your goal which is achievable but difficult.

CHAPTER: 3

WORK IS NOT THE CAUSE OF YOUR STRESS

Father: What do you think about intoxication?

Son: It is the condition of having lost some control of your action or behaviour under the influence of drug. It is not a good habit. I don't like people who consume drugs or alcohol because they don't have control over themselves.

Father: what is their state of mind during that time?

Son: They think they are in good mood, they are flying, they don't bother anyone.

Father: Yes, you are correct. I also enjoy that state of mind when I am intoxicated.
Son: But you don't consume alcohol?

Father: Intoxication is not only due to alcohol or drugs. When you enjoy some work by doing whether it is reading, playing, writing, painting, singing, or dancing. Imagine that you have a great love for playing the piano, and it is something that you feel passionate about. Throughout the day, you cannot stop thinking about it. Even when you are with your friends or at work, your mind is preoccupied with the thought of playing the piano as soon as you get home. When you are deeply passionate about something, you don't feel tired or drained by it because it energizes you instead.

I'll use myself as an example. These days, I am passionate about writing a book. I spend my days at the project site from 8 AM to 7 PM, performing routine tasks. However, I eagerly await returning home to start writing. Despite working the whole day, I do not feel exhausted. If you are intoxicated for something, you forgot to eat, drink, and sleep.

I would like to add something about work-life balance and productivity. The topic of work-life balance is quite extensive, but unfortunately, the concept is often misunderstood due to our laziness. People tend to view it as a contrast, where work and personal life are separate and mutually exclusive. However, this is not the case.

It seems that many of us lack motivation in our lives. Let's consider an example: when an employee is asked to work an additional hour by their boss after 5 PM, they may become disheartened and express dissatisfaction with their company and boss. However, if that same employee wanted to go shopping or see a movie after 5 PM, they may suddenly become energized and happy, without feeling tired. Where does this motivation come from? It comes from within, as nobody taught them how to feel motivated.

Cause of Stress

The factor causing stress are mainly due to:

1. No motivation at work.
2. No subject knowledge.
3. Lack of self-confidence.
4. Waste thoughts.
5. Living in the past and future.

For motivation, we need to look for the following things-

- Knowledge about the subject and understanding.
- Courage to take initiative.
- Will power.
- Self-confidence.
- Satisfaction.
- Feeling of progress and self-development.

You should love your work and workplace. You need to ask yourself every day what I am contributing to my organization. Have I done anything today to be proud of myself? When we record a new song, the earlier song is erased. Similarly, we need to re-program our subconscious mind for new aims, thoughts, and habits.

One should have willpower, knowledge of work, and initiative.

Son: "It's interesting to explore the concept of work-life balance. I have a question - why don't people choose a profession that gives them a sense of enjoyment? This way, work could be more like play, and they could earn money while doing something they love. What do you think about this idea?"

Father: Explore your inner interests and turn your passion into a source of income. Discover activities that bring you excitement and a sense of purpose to find fulfilling long-term goals and career paths. Take the time to identify your hobbies and pursuits that give you a sense of intoxication.

Son: From my experience, people usually don't use the word "busy" when they talk about their hobbies. It's just not a word that comes to mind when we're doing something we enjoy.

Father: Definitely, they don't say I am 'Busy' because they are 'Easy' while doing interesting work. So replace the word BUSY with BE EASY. If a person is not easily doing the work. It means he is not passionate about work, and it's like wearing a tight shirt and will feel like bondage. An intoxicated person will be happy and will keep flying. I remember a good saying "Do right, Be light".

Son: Wouldn't life be easier if you never felt tired?

Father: Life is not meant to be a constant struggle, but rather to be enjoyed. It is said that "Jahan Mohabbat hai wahan Mehnat nahi", which means that if there is love, there will be no need for effort. However, this doesn't mean that you shouldn't work hard. Instead, you should approach your work with love and dedication as if it's going to be a masterpiece that nobody has ever created before. It is said that stress is often a result of bad companionship. Life does not provide an academic degree, but it certainly puts you through the toughest exams and teaches you how to live.

"Life is a journey, and if you fall in love with the journey, you will be in love forever." - Peter Hagerty

Son: Bad company! What do you mean?

Father: Did you know that there are companies out there that are considered to be bad? Here's a list of some examples.

1. Your own habits and Sanskaras, which stop you from doing good things.
2. Your friends who are not motivated, who drain your energy.
3. Your wasted thoughts.
4. If you are in the present moment. Engaging your mind either in the past or in the future.
5. Using multiple electronic devices such as mobile phones, laptops, and televisions.
6. Social media.

POWERFUL BRAKE

When the project is going very smoothly, then you require a powerful brake to prepare for future crises.

Son: Doesn't it harm the progress by putting brake on progress and damage the confidence of team members?

Father: You don't need to put brake on others. I mean, a project manager need not be happy while it is progressing. You need to stop thinking the way others are thinking because nobody is going to think differently except you at this moment. You need to think in a different way asking questions to yourself like-

a. Is the project ongoing according to quality?
b. Is the process followed correctly?
c. What is the risk involved?
d. Any mistakes will give a non-confirmative, which will spoil the name and progress, which will cause rework and additional costs.

Now, you are required to ask yourself-

a. What is the other way to do the task?
b. How can productivity be improved?
c. How the resources can be minimized?

The myth is my work is the cause of my stress.

CHAPTER: 4

THE BIGGEST POWER- POWER TO TOLERATE

Father: What is power?

Son: I believe that having the ability to control your own actions or influence the actions of others is what defines power.

Father: What do you think about what are the powers a Project manager should have?

Son: I think he should have powers such as

a. Controlling and ruling power to control his team.
b. Able to face the challenges.
c. Power to decide and give orders.
d. Power to do anything he wants.
e. Coercive Power- to fire the person whenever you want.

Father: Most people believe these are powers, but I'll share what powers are truly essential.

Power

1. **Power to Tolerate-** A person can manage any difficult situation, and not be affected by the situation. There will be challenges internal and external. This is the most powerful power of a person. One can live his life happily without any conflicts. Tolerate means you must be cool or at peace. It doesn't mean just not speaking or reacting. It means you need to respond in such a manner that the other person doesn't get hurt. Includes: tolerating bad words, or bad atmosphere. Because of toleration power, one will be happy, and he will be powerful, looking braveness in his face, not weakness. Those who tolerate power will be more powerful. He will be happy. Tolerance means strength or inner power. **Tolerance means working under high pressure.** The manager must work in many similar situations simultaneously, which can create high pressure. He will get the feedback from all the situations and then decide. He must take all the

responsibility for the decision. He will bear criticism without any reaction or without being affected by the criticism.

Best example- Tree gives shadow to those who throw the stones to hit the fruit.

Tolerance comes from love. Tolerance means give. Tolerance means accepting both fame and defamation.

Do you consider yourself to be the embodiment of success? To be the embodiment of success, what main virtue is it essential to imbibe? To be the embodiment of success, you need the main virtue of tolerance. Tolerance and easiness will make any task successful. Just as when a patient person carries out a task after careful consideration and so receives success, in the same way, those who are tolerant can make those who have strong bitter Sanskars cool or make a difficult task easy with the power of their tolerance. Those who have the power of tolerance will also definitely be deep and mature. Those who are mature go into the depths, and those who go into the depths will never be afraid of any task. They will attain success by going into depth.

Those who have the power of tolerance will not allow either the vibrations of extroversion or the thoughts that are created in the mind to confuse them or make them afraid. With their power of tolerance, they will be able to face that also. What is visible from the face of those who have the virtue of tolerance? The faces of those who have the virtue of tolerance constantly reveal them to be content. Their eyes and features will never be those of discontentment. So those who themselves remain the embodiment of contentment will make others content, and whilst walking and moving, they will be experienced as angels. The virtue of tolerance is a very important dharna. The more you see the power of tolerance within yourself.

Accordingly, you should consider yourself to be content with yourself, and others to be content with you. To be content means to attain success. Some can tolerate anything: to tolerate something means to go into the depths of it. Just as when you go to the bottom of the ocean, you emerge with jewels, in the same way, those who are tolerant go into the depth, and through this depth, they can attain many powers. Only those who are tolerant can attain the power of churning. Those who are tolerant will constantly remain busy in their own internal churning. And those who are engaged in churning have a stage where they are lost in love. The power of tolerance is very essential. Their faces will be the embodiment of virtues. You have to pay this much attention to the inculcation of tolerance. Only those who are tolerant can be detached observers.

For example, a little straw doesn't break during a storm. Rises again when the storm is over. This power gives a manager or employee power for job rotation, changes in places, and changes in responsibilities.

How to increase the power of tolerance: We need to be flexible. When our body is flexible, we don't feel pain while bending. We need to mould our habits and Sanskar, the same as the body.

Tolerance is True Bravery.

2. **Power to Accommodate/ Adjust-** The power to accommodate is the ability to accept the presence, ideas, nature, and desires of others.

   Think of water for a second. It can take on any shape, just like it's trying to fit in with the container poured into, we too tend to adapt ourselves to fit into different situations. One of the most significant teachings we can learn in life is how to interact with and accommodate others in various situations. It involves developing the ability to accept people for who they are, without judgment or prejudice, and finding ways to adapt to their needs and preferences. This skill requires patience, compassion, and the willingness to put ourselves in other people's shoes. It also involves being open-minded and flexible, ready to adjust to different personalities, cultures, and beliefs, by learning to mix and adjust with others. By following this approach, we can establish more robust relationships, cultivate mutual respect, and foster a harmonious and inclusive environment. We all are unique. This power teaches us to be flexible in life. So, the manager gives way to others, able to bend and tolerate. The more flexible, the more pressure can be absorbed.

A teacher once gave a pot to his student and asked him to fill it up with water, sand, stones, and pebbles. However, there was a condition that none of the materials should fall outside of the pot. The student tried several combinations but was unsuccessful. Then the teacher explained to him that he should first fill the pot with stones, then pebbles, sand, and water. The moral of the story is that we should behave like the pot and adjust ourselves in any situation. We should use our strengths properly and in the right way.

How to imbibe: We should have love for others in our hearts to imbibe this power.

3. **Power to Discriminate-** This is our ability to 'separate' what is true from what is false; to differentiate between things.
   What is right and What is wrong? This is the most basic question that comes across while making a decision, whether small or big. Only when we discriminate between them can we make the right decision, can't we? Even with the two right ways, we may need to decide the best way. This is indeed a deep reflection of our human birth, that we can make

conscious decisions, decide our doings, and thus shape our future.

But a manager requires a lot of information, scrutiny, analysis, and knowledge to discriminate.

And why are you not able to distinguish? It is because you are not free from negative thoughts. Because of having wasteful or negative thoughts in your intellect. because your intellect is not clear, you are not able to discriminate. And, because of not being able to distinguish, you are not able to find a solution. Because of not being able to find a solution, you become influenced by something else.

How to imbibe: Keep your mind clean, waste though.

4. **Power to Judge-** This is the ability to assess our choices, decisions and actions in ourselves and in others.

   Judge means to "decide" what is right and what is wrong. When we judge ourselves, it is an opportunity to change, and not to repeat the same mistake next time. When we practice this, we are subconsciously shaping our intellect. We are telling our minds and senses what it is right to do. It is also a power to judge other people's character and thus avoid getting into a relationship with the wrong person or avoid being cheated.

   How to imbibe: You have to have a clear mind to imbibe this power.

5. **Power to Face-** The power to face is the capacity to face and resolve outer and inner barriers, tests, and challenges.

   Power to face challenges & people's negative behavior. This is one step further than Power to tolerate. On one side, we can tolerate the wrong and on the other side, we convey the truth that we hold, but in a peaceful way. This is the power to face difficulties in life. Be fearless and cross the obstacles.

This power only comes when there is 'truth' in our hearts, our actions are righteous, and we don't have any desire. "Agar Kaamna hai to Saamna nahi kar sakte" Honesty increases the power to face.

How to imbibe: When there is truth in our hearts, and our actions are righteous.

6. **Power to Co-operate-** This is our ability to give attention, time, experience, and wisdom in the service of others and to work alongside them. Helping others to go ahead or overcome their weaknesses or life challenges. When we are in a group working for a common purpose, we all need the power to accommodate and cooperate. We all have a role to play in this world drama, so it's important to stay humble and work well with others. Leave your ego at the door and you'll do just fine!
   The huge task can be made easy and enjoyable with the power to cooperate and create a spirit of teamwork.
   How to imbibe: Become egoless, remain humble and only then you will adjust and cooperate with everyone.

7. **Power to Withdraw-** It's our ability to step back and detach from the world around us for a minute or two. Detachment means being aware that I am separate from my body, roles, and responsibilities. The greater the ability to separate from external factors/ influences and maintain stability in all conditions, the higher the ability to handle problems. In this way, we will see things from the right perspective, make correct decisions, and not cause pain or suffering to others. Let us be aware: in my soul, I play the role of parent, spouse, child, etc. My job is just a way to make money and support myself and my family. Regardless of my role, my inherent nature is peace, love, purity, and happiness. I respect all other souls in the world. These qualities need to be demonstrated

in all my roles. I am a soul and I interact with other souls in different roles. We are all "actors" in this great global drama. When a manager has the power to withdraw, **he listens to someone what he is saying**. If he does not listen, he will assume based on his impression. If he doesn't listen, it will be a dangerous situation for the organization as he will not be able to assess the situation and decide. A manager should have the patience to hear someone. The best example of this power is the Tortoise. The behavior of a tortoise, using it metaphorically to describe a tendency to withdraw or be more reserved when not actively engaged in something. While tortoises are known for their slow and deliberate movements, the metaphorical usage may suggest a pattern of being more active or social when there's a specific purpose or task at hand and withdrawing or being more introverted when not engaged.

8. Power to Pack up: This is our capacity to finish things and to stop inefficient reasoning. Ability to stop a negative idea, word, or activity right away. Get together and push forward immediately. This power requires the act of "separation". We step back to get comfortable in our minds or hearts. We want to live the same life every day. Yet, "change" is to be sure the law of nature. Hence we should rehearse this ability to assemble what we presently have and push forward throughout everyday life. This is the force of mental capacity. Whenever he is called upon, he needs to pack up all other thoughts and pull out from whichever engagement his mind is busy in order to be fully available for the next.

When a soldier goes onto the battlefield without all of his equipment, and at the time of need he lacks even an ordinary weapon: because he lacks even that, there is damage caused. So here, too, you need to have all the powers working together: that is, you need to have all your weapons. With your intellect, you may be judging that something is ordinary, but even that ordinary matter deceives you when the time comes.

He must be available to those for whom he is responsible. Being ready means being always ready so you can start anything at any time. This means you have enough resources to delegate to others. If you can't delegate things, you're not well organized.

The myth is the biggest power is Controlling and Ruling power.

CHAPTER: 5
MIND MANAGEMENT

Son: What is Mind Management?

Father: This is the most important as our mind controls our life. One who learns to manage his mind has control over himself and can manage time and handle the work without stress.

Son: There will be thoughts coming and going. Can we control our minds also?

Father: Yes of course.

A simple practice of mind management:

- Live in the present moment- not in the past or future. Letting go involves living in the present rather than dwelling on the past. Focus on what you can control and create a positive future.
- Remove all distractions.
- Positive thoughts
- When faced with a challenge and you can't seem to find the answers, take a moment to tap into the incredible power of your subconscious mind. Center yourself and allow your thoughts to go beyond space and time, into the depths of your inner being. Trust that within you lies the solution you seek and ask your subconscious mind to reveal it to you. Remember, the energy of your thoughts is incredibly powerful and can shape your reality, so focus on positivity and intention as you connect with this incredible force within.

When our conscious mind ceases to work, our subconscious mind takes over and provides solutions. God has made the laws and gone to sleep. God has no role and no interest in fulfilling your desires. Your motive behind the desire is the most important than the desire itself. Instead of saying Oh God Please save us, you must say I am safe and protected. I will tell you the two incidents of my life to think about how the subconscious mind works-

Incident #1

I worked in a remote area 30 km away from Bangalore city. One Sunday, I visited an exhibition on building materials in Bangalore. At the exhibition, I came across a stall that sold Vaastu items such as wind chimes, feng shui products, pyramids, pebble stones, books, and bamboo sticks. The stall fascinated me, and I spent some time exploring the various items on display.

I entered the stall and just looked at the things kept over there. There was a white plastic pyramid. As a curiosity, I asked about that pyramid. The shop owner told me- it is a wish pyramid.

I asked him- Wish Pyramid!!! What does it mean?

Shop owner- He opened the pyramid in two parts, i.e., base and top pyramid shape cover. A dome-like cup of brass metal was fitted at the base of the pyramid. He showed me how to use this pyramid. He instructed to jot down your dream using 2-3 words on a 9" x 9" paper with a red ink pen, fold it four times, place it under the brass cup, and then close the top cover.

The pyramid should only be opened once your wish has come true. You need to keep this pyramid on your left hand and cover it with the palm of your right hand. You need to visualize your dream or wish in a picture form with closed eyes. It would help to frame a picture in your mind as your wish already has come true. This pyramid must be kept in your worship or meditation room.

I bought the pyramid at a significantly lower price.

I bought a new red ink pen from the market, nicely wrote my wish as "JOB IN XXXX Company," and portrayed a picture in my mind as I was at the construction project site wearing a helmet with the sticker of the company name XXXX. I am standing at the front of my site; there is a large excavation around 20 m deep; 3-4 excavators are working; in some places, reinforcement steel and foundations are already

Stress= Pressure/ Resilience

Father: Yes, you are absolutely right. Pressure refers to external factors and situations such as jobs, work, relationships, lifestyles, wealth, and so on.

Resilience refers to our inner strength, action, power, qualities, and so on.

On the numerator side, we don't have control over situations. We can't stop them. The situations have to come. We have full control over the denominator, which is our values, principles, and inner strength.

With the global pandemic affecting our lives, immunity has become a major topic of discussion. There is a wealth of information available on how to boost our immune system and what factors can affect it. From diet and lifestyle changes to exercise and stress reduction techniques, people have been exploring different ways to improve their immunity. Despite the challenges we've faced, there has been a renewed focus on maintaining good health and building resilience.

In today's world, stress has become a ubiquitous and ever-growing problem. It can be likened to a pandemic, as it affects millions of people worldwide and can have dire consequences on an individual's physical and mental well-being. However, instead of viewing it as a threat, many people consider stress to be a sign of their success and hard work, a badge of honor that they wear with pride. To combat this issue, it is essential to cultivate inner resilience and mental fortitude, which can help us cope with stress and prevent it from taking over our lives.

The myth is stress can be reduced by reducing external pressure only.

CHAPTER: 6
TIME MANAGEMENT

Son: Time keeps on moving. How can we control it?

Father: A finance manager manages the finances of big corporates. We look for better investment and saving plans for personal finance to get a good return. We need to give importance to managing time. We keep saying that time is money, but we have yet to treat time as money. We spend a lot of time making money and calculating interest; that is the cause of all our worries. The subject of time management is limited to one's interest and the subject of training. We should have a position as TIME ANALYST or TIME ACCOUNTANT in any organization.

We take care of so much of our wallets. But for time, we are spending like we have in abundance. For instance, if someone asks us what we're doing tonight, we might reply that we have no plans and can hang out or gossip. However, despite having enough time for leisure, we fail to dedicate time for personal growth such as learning new skills or putting in extra effort for our job that pays for our livelihood.

Son: What is the benefit of time management? I think It is a good reason for not doing work and giving excuses for not having time.

Father: A Good time management skill improves the quality of work and increases productivity. If a person fails to manage his time, he will be stressed out. Control time by using it well.

Benefits of time management:

- Happy and stress-free life
- People are creative.
- Absent rate is lower.
- Turnover rate is lower.
- Productive employee.

Challenges of Time Management:

- Procrastination.
- No motivation

- Being disorganised
- Don't want to change habits.
- Waste thoughts

Myth for Time Management:

- I don't have time due to workload.
- I am not getting support from the company.
- I know everything.

Tips for time management:

- Wake up at 4 PM.
- Start your day with positive thoughts.
- Meditation.
- No outside world news till 8 AM.
- Plan your activity of the day in the morning.
- Make do to list, prioritize, assign required time to complete.
- Keep track of daily tasks.
- Restrict time on Social media. Restrict consuming content.
- Manage "MIND"
- become conquerors of sleep

Conquer the Sleep

Son: Conqueror of Sleep? How to conquer the sleep. We need to have 8 hours of sleep every day, right?

Father: This is the myth that you need 8 hours of sleep. Sleep depends on various factors such as:

- Kind of food you consume- If you are consuming more spicy food, then you need more water to drink, say about 3 liters a day. If you consume less spice then you don't need 8 hours for sleep. You can try increasing your consumption of liquids or fruits in your food content, and then you will see the changes in your body that you are not tired after long hours of work, and you don't require 8 hours of sleep.

- Quantity of food- The more you eat, the more sleep you need. One should be eating half of the quantity of your hunger. Also, one should not eat more when one's favourite tasty food is on the table. It is said- Pure diet, Pure Mind.
- Way of eating- If you are eating your food in a hurry, it will take more time to digest as you are giving the work to your stomach what work teeth are supposed to do. Also, before starting to eat, you should give positive vibrations to your food and pay gratitude to the former who helped to grow the grains, the transporter who brought the grain to the mill, the nature who supported the grain to grow, the grain shopkeepers, the cook who prepared the food.

Son: That's all about food, I listen. Is there another way to conquer sleep?

Father: Sleep depends on what kind of energy we are consuming in a day. Such as-

- If we consume negative energy the whole day, we feel tired and require more sleep.
- If our screen time is more, spending more time on social media, we feel tired and require more sleep.
- If we sleep late at night and don't wake up early in the morning, we require more time to sleep.
- If we don't sleep in a completely dark room, the hormone called melatonin is not released, and we don't feel like enough sleep at night. So, it is advised to sleep in a dark room without any low-voltage bulbs so that you get enough sleep at night, as darkness releases enough melatonin.
- You recharge yourself in the morning with meditation and positive thoughts as we recharge our mobile and ensure it works full day without interruption. This

will enable us not to deplete our energy till night, and thus, we don't require 8 hours of sleep in the night.

- Exercising is the way to keep your body healthy and fit for the purpose of your life. If we are not healthy, we will be wasting a lot of time visiting the hospital and wasting money. A healthy body requires less sleep.

These are all ways to reduce your sleep time and get more time for the day. This is one of the methods for saving time. However, consuming caffeine or pills to reduce sleep time is not advisable.

There are several successful people in the world who sleep 4 to 6 hours a day, such as Marissa Mayer- CEO of Yahoo, Narendra Modi- Prime Minister of India, Jack Dorsey- Twitter founder and Square CEO, Indra Nooyi- Chairman and CEO of PepsiCo, and Tim Cook- CEO of Apple2.

Son: You mean we should force ourselves to reduce sleep time day by day?

Father: It doesn't mean, you have to force yourself to reduce your sleep. But slowly, you need to reduce with some incremental, let's say, by about 10 min every month. At the same time, you have to make sure you are not putting any burden on your body. You should not fall sick. If we are hungry or thirsty, our body gives a signal to us. In the same way, our body gives a signal to rest or sleep, but we override the signal and prefer to take tea or coffee or any other method to control our sleep. It is up to you to decide now whether you want to sleep or recharge with 5 minutes of deep meditation or Yog Nidra. It is the same as charging your mobile battery.

The best method to increase your energy level is to keep your body healthy.

Son: Everybody knows the Pomodoro technique that you need to take 10-minute breaks every 50 minutes of work. But we don't follow due to workload.

Father: This is also a good method to recharge ourselves. There is another method that I strongly recommend you follow. Take a break of 5 minutes every hour just to be in silence. Withdraw all your thoughts from the outer world just to be with you; meditate for 5 minutes, and you will be recharged for the next hour. You try this practice for two weeks to see any changes in your mental status. If you don't feel any significant gain, then definitely you can stop.

The myth is I don't have time.

CHAPTER: 7
25 Hours in a day.

There are certain works that are not required to take any action at the present movement. Some team members are very much concerned about that the work to be completed right now, as they want to tick the number of tasks are being finished.

Son: Some people understand some work to be completed first, and others think it should be completed later. What do you think, which work should be done first? And who will decide?

What is Priorities

Father: These things are to be aligned with the team members depending upon the goal and vision of the company. The work which has the highest impact on the result. This achieves common objectives. The focus with time and resources towards a particular work and creating greater results to achieve a common goal is the Priority.

This is very important for time management and project management, where a manager adjusts all his resources to complete the task.

Disadvantages of not setting priorities

Son: It seems the whole project depends on priorities.

Father: Whether you are managing a project or you are handling any situations in life. You must follow the process of setting priorities. Priorities are the key to success in life.

Whenever you are overloaded with a set of tasks in your life, you feel crazy about it and don't understand which work to be completed first. You get confused. You might have seen such a person in life that they will be busy doing something but still not able to complete the work. They seem to be lost in their work. They are frustrated with the work. They are found in the workplace with anger, worry, and stress because they are not organized. These kinds of people can be seen in every office.

They will not only think that I am the only one working in the office, but they will also believe that everyone else is just lounging around and gossiping. On top of that, they will blame the management for not giving them a decent raise compared to other employees.

Son: What are the disadvantages of not setting priorities in life?

Father: I will tell you; there are a lot of drawbacks.

1. Output is less.
2. Improper utilization of resources
3. Improper utilisation of time
4. No team spirit.
5. Common goal is not achieved.
6. No teamwork.
7. No work/life balance.
8. No interest in work.
9. Working in stressed as important works are incomplete.
10. Deadlines are missing.
11. The project is not on track.
12. Not able to manage workload.
13. No quality works.
14. Rework
15. Cost overruns.

How to set Priorities

Father: Now you understand the importance of setting priorities. There are the above-mentioned things that need to be avoided. Thus, priority setting is very important.

Son: It seems that setting priorities is a very complicated task.

Father: No, not at all. It is very simple and can be implemented very easily. You just need to understand the company's objectives and vision. A certain set of activities might be a priority in some companies, and it may not be a priority in other companies. One needs to understand here. The person needs to change themselves here. They might have a lot of experience in doing certain things and want to implement the same working methodology in some other company, which may not work because of the vision or objectives of that company.

Here comes frustration when his ego has been tested. His working methodology is being aligned with a new company, and again, he feels discomfort with other team members. The person should be flexible enough to change himself and adopt a new culture according to the requirements of the organization.

The priorities also change if the objectives get changed within the same organization. If a person learns to set his priorities, he won't be stressed and will be doing his work happily.

Steven Coven has suggested keeping tasks in four quadrants-

a. Important and urgent works

   The problem, Crises, and deadlines come under the category of important and urgent works, which require immediate action and, if not acted upon on time, will negatively affect the organization. These activities are always on a critical path.

b. Important but not urgent works

   This is mostly related to long-term goals. These are important but not urgent, such as relation building, finding new opportunities, long-term planning, personal growth and recreation, etc.

c. Not important but urgent works

   This is mostly routine work like sending mail; calls fall into this category; it will not have more of an impact on our lives.

d. Not important not urgent works

Activities in this category should be avoided or ignored. You can save a lot of time and be productive. Activities in this category include watching TV, spending time on the Internet, gossiping, etc.

20% of your time is to be used for quadrant 1, and 80% of your time is to be used for quadrant 2. The daily and weekly tasks are required to be listed in one place and check which one is most urgent and will be our priority of work to be completed.

Time management and Priority Management

Son: I think the meaning of both time management and priority management is the same and interchangeable according to the type of work. Am I correct?

Father: There are significant differences in both. Now you need to understand it.

Time management is planning your time to be assigned for the activity in a day to produce maximum output. You can have control over the activity and can ensure that no time is wasted on a particular time and it is completed within time.

Priority management is putting activities that need to be completed first in preference. The activity that produces maximum impact is kept on priority. It is a very important factor to be considered in day-to-day life. After prioritizing, we need to assign time to the activity. Thus, first, we need to do priority management, and then time management comes into the picture.

25 hours in a day

Son: What if the work assigned to the activity is not being completed on time?

Father: If one cannot complete the task on time, then one needs to recheck whether the time assigned to this task is realistic, whether there is an issue in the methodology of doing it, or whether some other factors are impacting the activity.

Son: You have mentioned a lot of things for setting priorities, and still, I feel we don't have enough time in a day to complete the task. It is the same with other students who are staying in my hostel.

Father: How many hours in a day do you have?

Son: Of course, it is 24 hours. I have a perfect timetable for my daily routine, and I am not able to accommodate any additional work in my schedule.

Father: What if I will tell you that you have 25 hours in a day? What is your daily routine in general?

Son: I am really jam-packed with my daily schedule.

Father: But I want to know what kept you jam-packed. Will you be able to tell me?

Son: In general, 8 hours for sleeping, 5 hours in school, 1 hour for traveling, 3 hours for self-study, 1 hour for breakfast, lunch, and dinner, 1 hour for bath & getting ready, 1.5 hours for watching TV, 2 hours in social media, 1.5-hour playing.

Father: Now you give me some time from your daily routine. You are doing some activities that are really timewasters.

Can you reduce your time in some of the activities, such as 15 minutes from sleeping, 15 minutes from watching TV, 15 minutes from time-consuming social media, and 15 minutes from playing? It's all around 60 minutes. Now, how much total time have you saved? 1 hour. So, you have 25 hours in a day. This 1 hour you should spend in learning new skills.

Son: Oh, that's great; Our motto should be focused on saving time rather than solely concentrating on activities. You need to learn to steal time.

Father: Highly successful or rich people don't waste their time. They have their plan for every minute. Their schedule for the day is fixed. Can we also follow in our lives, or do we just want to be happy to see rich people?

STORY: The story illustrates a powerful lesson about mindset, responsibility, and the impact of one's approach to life. Two best friends studied together and went to other countries for jobs. They did not have connections for a long time. After so many years, the first friend applied for an interview and got a job in a well-known, reputed company. The first friend was introduced to the company's owner on the very first day.

He was surprised to see his friend as the owner of the same company. Both were very happy to see each other. They discussed their childhood times.

The first friend asked the other friend the secret of his success. The other friend replied it was all because of mindset. He reminded the first friend that they were going to college one day and asked if we forgot to switch off the room lights. You said to leave it; we are not required to return it as we pay the light bill. But you know what I did? I returned to the hostel, switched off the lights, and went to college. Those days also you had the worker's mentality, and I take ownership of this. That is why I am here, running a company, and you are an employee till today.

The friend who eventually became the company owner took responsibility for a small task like turning off the lights. This act reflects a mindset of ownership and a sense of responsibility, even for seemingly trivial matters. Small actions, such as turning off lights, may seem insignificant at the time. Still, they can have a cumulative impact on one's character and future opportunities. Consistently demonstrating responsibility in small matters can pave the way for more significant responsibilities.

The myth is I am utilizing my time properly and I am Busy.

CHAPTER: 8

DON'T ASK FOR A CAPABLE, HARD-WORKING EMPLOYEE, WHO CAN WORK UNDER PRESSURE

Son: For the successful completion of the project, I think every manager will be looking for the best team members. I have seen the advertisement for job openings describing academic and general qualifications.

Father: It is correct also and I agree that the system is being followed. I have seen many schools and colleges asking for top students for their colleges or universities, and they are claiming that their universities are ranking at this number. Is it correct?

Son: What is the harm in there? I don't think there is any problem in asking the rankers' students.

Father: Then who owns the responsibility of developing those students who are not performing well? The great thing is not in producing results with the perfect candidates (all favourable conditions). Instead, the greatness is in producing results in adverse conditions.

Son: I think you are right to some extent.

Father: We are taking everything from this universe. We are the human beings who are taking only. When are we going to give back and pay the returns? Now, I think it is our social responsibility to give to the world what we know and what skills we have and extend a hand of support to those who are incapable of producing the required results. In the previous chapter, you might have learned about the power of the subconscious mind. Now, I would like to tell you the secret of the law of attraction.

Our Though Creates Vibration

Son: What is this law?

Father: Whatever we think, it creates a vibration, and this vibration radiates to the universe. These vibrations also work with Newton's third law of motion.

You might have seen when you throw a ball against a wall, the ball applies a force on the wall. Likewise, the wall also applies force on the ball resulting in the ball bouncing off the wall. Similarly, a gravitational force is working on Earth to pull us. We are not realizing it because we are exerting a force of the same amount on the earth.

We are energy beings. Whatever energy we are sending to the universe will manifest and will come to us.

What is our general perspective on a person who is not performing well? We send negative vibrations such as:

- He is always making mistakes.
- I knew already he would not improve.
- Nobody can make him understand what we want?
- He is very lazy and doesn't want to work.
- We can't trust him.

Also, if you are sending negative thoughts to a person who is already dull or underperformer. Then what will happen? Your vibrations will bring them down further, and he will not be performing well even if he is trying to overcome his deficiencies. Your negative vibrations will stop him from overcoming his deficiencies.

Son: Our vibrations are affecting others? It is very surprising.

Father: We need to send positive vibrations to him and change our perspective towards him being a merciful person and create the thoughts like:

- He is doing good.
- He is improving a lot.
- We should trust him.

One more important thing to note is that wherever the eye goes, the energy flows. If we see a deficiency in others, it will deplete our energy and attract the deficiency only and this deficiency can be transferred to us as well. So, we should be looking at the qualities in others and utilize them.

Team Development

Your team is the pieces in the showcase. You need to keep attractive and active pieces in the showcase. You have to be very easy in nature.

Son: What if, even after your support and guidance, they are unable to produce the required results?

Father: We need to assess the quality and characteristics of the staff and follow Field Marshal Moltke's Matrix.

As per the matrix-

Field Marshal Moltke's Four Officer Attribute Matrix

Intelligence \ *Initiative*	Lazy	Energetic
Smart	**Commanders** Make the Right Things Happen but in the Easiest Possible Manner (Discover)	**General Staff Officers** Direct the Right Things to Happen (Capture)
Dumb	**Menial Tasks** Follow Orders to Perform Routine Tasks that must be Done by an Officer (Maintain)	**Eliminate** Will Make Things Happen – but the Wrong Things (Destroy)

Moltke places the Smart & Lazy office as his Commanders because they find the right way of doing things in less time. They should be in a higher position in any organization.

He used to place Smart and energetic General Staff Officers in his office because they are good at making intelligent plans and making the right things happen. Poor leaders can be promoted up to a certain level; they can see orders are being carried out.

He used to place Dumb and lazy officer for their routine work that they could accomplish, and they followed orders without causing much harm. They were given simple, repetitive, and unchallenging tasks to perform.

He used to eliminate Dumb and energetic officers because they may cause danger to the organization. They can do any wrong thing at any time. This kind of people may destroy the system and can be harmful to the organization.

As the matrix suggests the people who fall under the fourth box should not be kept in the organization, should be eliminated, or terminated.

Son: Is this the only solution?

Father: No. At this point, I do not agree with the matrix. This kind of people should not be removed from the organization. If you do so, then what is the difference between you and that university that doesn't accept underrated students?

This is the point that took me a long time to realize, and I advocate encouraging such type of person. In our family, if our child is not performing well in academics or he may be physically / mentally weak, what do we do? We support, encourage, and care for them. So, in the same way here, we also need to be merciful towards him.

We should be giving him such work according to his capacity, and we also need to guide him, educate him, and empower him with new skill development. If an employee is weak in his performance, and we want to give him feedback about his performance, it is a tricky thing. We have to tell the truth, also keeping in mind that his moral is not hampered. We have to be polite and diplomatic when sharing a negative trait to a person. Like a mouse that cuts the person to bleed without letting the person feel. This quality will help the person change without effecting a person self-respect.

You should extend all your support to him. In any organization, if a new employee joins or any employee is not good at work, they need guidance and support for some time till he gets stabilized.

Hero of the Project

Do you consider yourself to be a leading actor, a hero actor, in this elevated drama? Everyone's attention is always on the main actors. So, do you act while considering yourself at every second to be a leading actor? Famous actors have three things. What are these? Firstly, they will be active. Secondly, they will be accurate. And thirdly they will be attractive. Famous actors have these three things. So, do you consider yourself to be a famous or leading actor in this way?

Those who are active can mould themselves in whatever way and at whatever time they want: they can adopt that form at any time.

Your thoughts should always be accurate regardless of the situation, discipline, code of conduct, or contract.

Those who embody actual and elevated knowledge will also have the attraction. Physical beauty can only attract you when someone comes close to you, or in front of you, but this attraction can attract others who are sitting at a distance.

Son: What about a Project Manager thinking about himself?

Father: A Project manager to consider yourself a hero of the project. He should have complete confidence in his team members. It will not happen in one day. Take baby steps. As you go ahead, you will see the next steps. Start with ZERO then progress towards ONE.
Now, can you list out the things a Hero does?

Son: 1. A hero should be Superman; he will be doing everything.

2. He should be strong, knowledgeful.

3. He should be helpful. Give hands to needful.

4. He will be in the front. He should be facing all the challenges.

5. He will be leading the team.

6. He has the solution to all the problems.

...and I think a Project Manager should have all these qualities as he is the leader of the Project.

Father: Yes, now you got the point. A Project Manager should be very close to these qualities; if he does not have them, he should be striving to achieve them. There are some practices and positive affirmations to imbibe the above qualities and gain confidence.

EXERCISE: Wake up in the morning and have positive affirmations-

1. I am the Hero of the Project.
2. My project is going very smoothly.
3. I have solutions for everything.
4. I have faith in me and in my team.
5. I believe in God; he is with me, and He is holding my hand.
6. All my staff are very good; they are performing well.

3 Certificates

Son: I think a Project Manager is required to be qualified and certified by some institute or university.

Father: Yes, definitely, but these certificates are not sufficient to be a perfect Project manager apart from experience in the relevant field.

Son: Who will be the issuing authority for these other certificates and what are all these certificates?

Father: A Project Manager has to get these certificates from 3 different places. First certificate from himself, second from his superior, and third from his team. Let's take them one by one.

How does he get the certificate from himself? He needs to ask himself some questions-

1. Am I doing my work honestly?
2. Am I honest with my company?
3. Am I content with my work?
4. Do I have enough knowledge to perform as a Project Manager?
5. Am I always support or encourage my team?

6. Am I ethical towards my work?
7. Am I not misusing my powers?

If the answer to all the above questions is YES, then you can give yourself a certificate. Someone might probably gather about 60 or 80 % marks in these questions, and then you can make an effort and improve yourself to achieve 100%.

The second one is getting certificates from your superior. A person needs to ask these questions to himself.

1. Are my superiors satisfied with my work?
2. Am I following their instruction?
3. Am I working as per the company's strategic priorities?

If the answer to all the above questions is YES, then you can get a certificate from the Superiors.

The third one is getting certificates from your team. A person needs to ask these questions to himself.

1. Am I merciful towards them?
2. Am I showing favoritism towards someone?
3. Am I supporting, encouraging, and guiding them?
4. Am I standing with them in case of criscs?

If the answer to all the above questions is YES, then you can get a certificate from the team. For the second and third certificates, if you think you are achieving 85% marks, then you can consider it 100% because 100 % of people will not be satisfied with you. Everyone's priorities and requirements are different; as a manager, you cannot fulfil all of their requirement. So, they will always be dissatisfied. You need not be worried about the rest of the 15% of people.

Son: These certificates are like self-checks. One can introspect himself. I think can apply this everywhere.

How To Be One Who Uplift Others

With the lenses we wear, we perceive the world. Team

development requires uplifting others who are not performing as anticipated. But who can uplift others:

1. One who uplifts others constantly sees other souls as embodiments of virtues.
2. When seeing the weaknesses or defects of anyone, one who uplifts others will see that defect with good wishes and feelings of cooperation and will donate power to make that soul virtuous.
3. One who uplifts others means to be one who constantly donates his own treasures.
4. those who uplift others are constantly full, they would not have the desire to give to others only after receiving something from them. They would never even have the thought that they will do something when that one does it: "I will change when the other one changes. That one should change a little and then I will change a little.
5. Instead of being great donors, they become businessmen who constantly make deals. "When that one gives this much, I will give this much."
6. For those with whom everyone else is disheartened, they would ignite lamps of hope for those people who are in such a state.

STORY: I dedicate this story to those parents and teachers who want their pupils to play in school competitions and social gatherings.

"The game of musical chairs"- I think everybody played this game not only in his childhood but also at office refreshment parties and other social functions.

11 participants and 10 chairs. The music is played, and 11 participants will move around; when the music is stopped, the participants will sit on the chair, and the one who cannot get the chair will be out of the game. And one chair was also removed. Now 10 participants and 9 chairs. The game continues like that; at the last round, there will be one chair

and 2 participants. The winner will be the person who gets the chair.

What we imbibe or learn from this game is that we need to think for ourselves, selfishness, self-centeredness, and no team building. The same person or child grows up and goes to work. The corporation invests heavily in team building and fostering cooperation among employees. However, the same child did not question how this differs from what they've been taught in school.

The same game is played in Japan also. The music is played. 11 participants move around the 10 chairs. As the music is stopped 10 participants will sit on the chair and one who did not get the chair is standing. Immediately the person who sitting on the chair close to him will allow him to sit with him on the same chair because the rule now is if anyone loses, everyone loses. Thus, nobody goes out of the game.

Now one chair is removed, the 11 participants and 9 chairs. Again, the music is played and the game continues. If all the participants can accommodate each other than the team is declared as winner. In this game, the participant's focus will be on others and others should not be out of the game.

The same game but a different attitude i.e. traditional version and modified version. The traditional version shows a sense of individual competition, self-preservation, and the concept that only one person can win. On the other hand, the Japanese version emphasizes cooperation, mutual support, and the idea that everyone succeeds or fails together. This cultural difference reflects broader societal values and norms related to teamwork, unity, harmony, and community well-being.

It's common for us to blame children for their behavior, attitudes, and etiquette, and to say that "kids these days" are just different. We compare them to our old customs, assuming that we were perfect. However, the story above is an example of how we often teach children the wrong things during their childhood and then expect them to change their behavior later on. It's important to recognize our own role in shaping children's behavior and to try to guide them in a positive direction.

The myth is we can get the work done only by capable employees. Also, a Smart and Energetic person should be in a higher position.

CHAPTER: 9
PROBLEM-SOLVING - FACING

THE CHALLENGES

Every lock has a key. So, there is a solution to every problem.

As we are going through quick, fragile, evolving times, there is no such day when we can say "OK." Today is a fine day. I did not find anything that came up, any issues, any circumstances, any heaviness, and any arguments.

Hence to get by, we really want to have a strong groundwork. However, where could I, at any point, track down a solid groundwork? The response is the source to re-energize me.

STORY: A man was dissatisfied with his life and wanted to live as a monk. He left his house and family and travelled far away from his city. He built a hut outside a small village and started his spiritual practice. Gradually, people from the village learned of his presence and his monastic lifestyle.

The story goes that a monk would often give discourses to the villagers. However, a rat would frequently cut his clothes, which annoyed him greatly. The villagers suggested that he keep a cat to scare the rat away, and they provided one for him. The monk then began to worry about how he would feed the cat. In response, the villagers suggested that he keep a cow, which would provide milk for the cat, and they also provided a cow for him. However, the monk was still concerned about who would take care of the cow. The villagers then suggested that he keep a mate to take care of the cow, and they provided one for him. As time passed, the monk realized he had unintentionally formed a family in the village while he had left his home to live alone. So, the problem is like that. One cannot go away from his problems. We need to deal with it.

What is Problem

Let us understand what the problem is. The problem or challenges are a situation, person, or thing that needs attention and needs to be dealt with or solved. Problems are external factors whose presence affects our state of mind, work, etc., and makes us uncomfortable. There are problems that come due to miscommunication in the team. Also, you must remember one thing: the problems will always be there outside we need to be stable from the inside.

You should consider the problem as

1. Test Paper
2. The challenges come to teach you a lesson. Don't be afraid, but just learn the lesson! Sometimes, it teaches the lesson of tolerance, and sometimes, the lesson of maintaining a constant and steady stable stage. Sometimes it comes to help you make the lesson of becoming an embodiment of peace firm.

What is Problem Solving Skills

At the beginning of the book, you have read the story of Boss and the military. In some situations, there is only one way to face challenges like in the story. But generally, you should be looking for option B to solve the problem.

Problem-solving skills are the skills to determine the root cause of the problem and find the possible solution.

What is Problem Solving Steps

The steps for problem-solving are-

1. Maintain a calm and positive mindset. Avoid feeling overwhelmed by the unfamiliarity of the problem. A positive attitude enhances your ability to think creatively and make sound decisions.
2. Define the Problem- Here, you will diagnose the problem with a cause-and-effect diagram.
3. Generate Alternative Solutions (Consider your past experience)
4. Evaluate and select alternative solutions.

   Assess the pros and cons of each potential solution. Consider factors such as feasibility, cost, impact, and potential risks. Eliminate options that are impractical or unlikely to address the problem effectively.

5. Implementation.
6. Reverse thinking: Consider the opposite of what you believe might be a solution. This approach can help you break away from conventional thinking and explore alternative perspectives.

What is the process of solving the Problem-

In order to face any obstacles, you first need the power of discrimination. Then, you need the power to make decisions.

When we diagnose the problem, we can only decide whether the solution brings temporary attainment or permanent attainment after making the decision.

In a school, some children are able to give the overall result, but when their teacher asks how they arrived at the result, they get confused, you should also know the method from which the outcome is derived. So which main aspect is essential to increase the power of making decisions? (Churning the ocean of knowledge.)

Son: Why does our brain become lazy and start to avoid thinking?

Father: It may be because of the following reasons:

1. When you take work from your brain more than required, and if you don't give rest, it may lead to stress. It shows difficulty in concentrating and a sense of mental exhaustion.
2. Lack of Sleep may cause a negative impact. The brain struggles to focus.
3. Boredom and lack of interest may contribute to mental laziness.
4. Information overload
5. Poor lifestyle.
6. Lack of motivation.
7. Fear of failure: Individuals may avoid thinking or acting in a way that avoids recognizing their mistakes.

Son: How can we improve our ability to troubleshoot and solve problems effectively?

Father: Yes, it's a good question. Below are the tips to become a better troubleshooter.

1. **Consider it a challenge:** Take the problem as a challenge, don't get disturbed. Put yourself in the driver's seat. Turn your obstacle into opportunity.

2. **Be Proactive:** To be proactive working, anticipate problems, and actively try to prevent them. For example, Let's say you have an important meeting, and your task for the meeting is to prepare a presentation about a project you are currently working on. As this is your first time presenting, you're not really sure how to prepare a presentation properly so you feel stuck.

   So what would a proactive person do in this situation?

   First, a proactive person wouldn't be afraid to admit they lack experience or skills and that they need help. The next step would be to ask your colleagues for advice — the sooner you ask, the better. This will prevent the whole team from wasting time on a presentation that's a failure. So, instead of unsuccessfully trying to complete the presentation yourself, the better option is to seek guidance. There's no shame in that.

   If you want to prevent problems and be proactive, you need to act in advance. To forestall issues and be proactive, you really want to act ahead of time.

3. **Be confident:** Your motivation increases when you are confident.

4. **Take responsibility:** Sometimes our plans fail and that's okay. It's a part of life. Successful people get up and try again. Look for lessons from every mistake or perceived failure. Be careful not to blame the other person because it makes you weaker.

5. **Don't complain:** Just start moving: Complaining uses a lot of energy, which is wasted in complaining, and it makes you feel uncomfortable. Suppose there are 3 meetings today. You should not complain about how many meetings you need to attend; start working on a time management solution.
6. **Learn from past experience:** Don't solve the problem alone. Use your past experience and ask the expert who has done this task before.

Do It Now Attitude

Do not say I will try and do it; say I will do it.

Advantages of the Do it Now attitude:

1. Breaks the cycle of procrastination.
2. Increases productivity.
3. Stops overthinking.
4. Accomplishes more in less time.
5. Solve many problems.
6. Improved mental health.
7. Feels Overwhelmed.
8. Reduces stress.

Son: How can I acquire do it now attitude?

Father: There are the following steps to acquire do it now attitude:

Create a Sense of Urgency. Unfortunately, we procrastinate and justify ourselves: "Why do today what can be put off until tomorrow?". We don't want to create a focus and a sense of urgency to complete a task today. We have turned into a society of procrastinators rather than doers. Those that are successful are so because they didn't wait until tomorrow. They are master implementers who always take action and move towards their goals. Create a sense of urgency and strive to do what you need to do today, not tomorrow. When in doubt and you find yourself asking the question, "When should I do …… (fill in the blank), the answer is simple: NOW.

When faced with the question, "When should I do...?" let the answer resound definitely: NOW. Recognize that the present moment is your most valuable asset. Every delay is a missed opportunity for progress.

Imagine the impact of completing tasks promptly. Picture the positive outcomes, the sense of accomplishment, and the momentum gained. Visualization can fuel the urgency needed to propel you into action.

Don't Think of Early Retirement

A significant number of us keep on longing to resign early. Retirement plans constrain individuals out of the labor force sooner than anticipated. The majority of people fantasize about their ultimate retirement. Who wouldn't want a permanent vacation—a completely new life—free from jobs, obligations, and stress?

Yet, retirement, by its very definition, means never again being useful. We resign old hardware, we resign old dress, and we resign old thoughts when they've quit filling a need … and we resign ourselves for a similar explanation. Don't say that you are of no use and don't think that you don't want to live now.

We live by purpose in the current modern world. If we don't have any purpose in life, we become dull and look old.

Instead, one should be having a bigger, exciting dream in his life, not a boring, smaller, predictable one. Retirement simply doesn't make sense if "a life of purpose is the purpose of life."

Retirement is associated with an increase in various adverse health outcomes as well as a loss in mobility and mental health. You will need to stretch out your retirement savings. Health insurance premiums also increase after age 50. The transition period is from a very busy routine life to retirement time. People miss their colleagues and bosses. That is another problem.

Being older means you have more experience and gain more than others. you need to continue the same way you are doing. When you're up in the game, why give up?

The myth is I can go away from the problem.

CHAPTER: 10
COMMUNICATION AND TRACKING

Father: Communication is the most crucial aspect of a project. Most of the project managers will be spending almost 80% of their time in communication.

There are two forms of communication- Verbal communication & written communication. Written communication has various forms like emails, letters, etc. The advantage of proper communication is:

- Reduces miscommunications.
- Increase happiness.
- Develop trust.
- Resolves many problems.
- Encourage collaboration.
- Builds friendship among team members.
- Improve productivity.

To-Do list

For proper communication, we need to prepare a certain list called a to-do list. The to-do list is generally used to manage time properly. In a whole day, week, or month, what the work we need to accomplish has to be noted down.

We also spent some time preparing a to-do list, and we found it very difficult to achieve the work as per the list. It is also causing stress as we need to update it, revise it, and prioritize it. I prepare a to-do list, but when the list goes more than one page, it creates an unnecessary burden to update.

Later, I started writing down the essential works on the whiteboard. Initially, it gave a lot of interest, but later on, when the items increased, a lot of unimportant work was also noted down. Then I stopped this also.

I used to write my to-do list on a yellow post-it note and stick it to the front of my table. However, this caused a lot of problems as sometimes I would miss important tasks if the post-it fell on the floor without me noticing.

After struggling to keep track of my to-do list, I decided to create an Excel spreadsheet. However, I sometimes forget to open it on my laptop, resulting in an outdated list.

After realizing that my to-do list can be tracked on the calendar, I began assigning specific times to each activity so that I could receive notifications as reminders.

After trying different methods based on my work, working style, and interests, I discovered my own way of making a to-do list. I simply note down my tasks on scratch paper and update it daily according to my progress.

It's a good idea to carry a pocket notebook to jot down important things. Many successful people, such as Richard Branson, have adopted this habit.

It is important to have both a to-do list and a diary. While the to-do list helps in keeping track of tasks, a diary can be used to document important decisions, tasks, and meeting minutes for future reference. One common problem with a to-do list is that we tend to prioritize easy and interesting tasks, even if they are not urgent. According to a report, the average worker spends approximately 2.9 hours on non-work activities during an 8-hour workday.

Son: What is the disadvantage of the to-do list?

Father: There are disadvantages also;

- Stress due to uncompleted tasks; people feel unsuccessful by the end of the day if the list shows incomplete tasks.
- People focus on quantity rather than quality.
- Feeling of guilt
- Neglect of long-term goals.
- A long list can be overwhelming and cause stress.

Emails

The most hectic task is checking all the emails we are receiving and replying to them on time. A manager has to spend a lot of time reading them, delegating, and writing replies to all the emails. How to get control over these. You can probably adopt these steps:

- Don't put notifications on your laptop; otherwise, you will be spending a lot of time reading and replying to emails. You can assign time for checking email, let's say every two hours, you will check your inbox. If you don't want to follow this, then it will distract you when a notification comes in between if you are doing some critical work.
- Unsubscribe unnecessary emails.
- Don't reply immediately to any emails. Take some time.
- Don't keep a copy of someone who has no contribution to the subject because it will just increase his mailbox size.
- Make a centralized system for replying. Not everyone is replying to any emails.
- One should be very particular about the subject line. Make sure it is easy to track or search after a year or two. The subject matters a lot.
- If you can talk to a person, then don't send email, if it is not required for record.
- There should not be any mail in your inbox that is unread by the end of the day. It requires hard work to maintain it, but I am able to do so.
- Also, It is very important to have a glance of yesterday's email at the beginning of the day to check and confirm that no important emails are missed out.

Meetings

Running a meeting is an important task for a project. But if two or more people meeting frequently on the table and can resolve the issues then meetings are not required to waste the time of all the attendees. A meeting is considered a waste of time, if –

- It has no agenda.
- If the meeting does not start on time.
- Attendees are coming late, not respecting the time.
- Unprofessional behavior of the attendees.
- Unnecessary people are called for meeting.
- If a meeting exceeds 45 to 60 minutes, and people are spending more time discussing the issues than necessary, then it is not an effective meeting. In such cases, the project requires serious attention, and it is best to resolve the issues in a different manner.
- 15 minutes daily huddle at site is not being done.
- People attend without homework.

Tracking

Whatever, be the mode of communication, if it is not tracked properly, it is going to be a disaster for a project. Every project needs to give more importance to this task.

There are several ways to track the communication. An electronic file as well as hard copy to be filed for all correspondences whether it is incoming or outgoing documents. A log containing incoming and outgoing list of communications corresponding to date to be prepared. There is no proper format for this, but it can be prepared as per requirements and project demands.

The tracking increases the efficiency of the workforce via increased productivity. The most important factor is that the tracking of the correspondence should be like so as its retrial should not be taking time.

The searching of documents wastes lot of time of an employee. The report says-

8 searches are done to find out one document.

Employees spend 1.5 hours (some sources say 2.5 hours) a day searching for documents. Or in another way, 4 employees work out of 5 and 5th one spends the whole day in searching the documents.

We are not going with the correctness of the data, but want to tell you the truth about how we can avoid wastage of time by keeping a proper document tracking system.

The myth is We should not spend more time and resources in tracking of communications.

CHAPTER: 11
MANAGING STRESS

"This life is yours. Take the power to choose what you want to do and do it well. Take the power to love what you want in life and love it honestly. Take the power to walk in the forest and be a part of nature. Take the power to control your own life. No one else can do it for you. Take the power to make your life happy."

--Susan Polis Schutz

We all desire for a smooth life, but it never seems to happen. Even a short ad on a 5-minute YouTube video can make us feel stressed. Imagine watching a movie where all the characters are happy and content throughout the entire story. Such a movie would be a complete failure because it would lack any conflict or drama.

When we watch a movie with a suspenseful and tragic villain, we enjoy it and it often becomes a box office success.

Let's sit back and enjoy the movie. Life is just like a movie full of twists and turns. It has its suspense, thrill, and tragedy. The good news is that you are the hero of your own movie. We all enjoy the villains in movies, but we don't want them in our lives. Unfortunately, the circumstances we face in life can be just as challenging as a villain. They can cause stress and pain. When someone is struggling, they don't necessarily need knowledge, but rather support. This empowers the person to think critically and make informed decisions.

Cause of Stress

There are various reasons why people experience stress. For instance, one person may enjoy washing their clothes, while another may feel overwhelmed by the task. The reasons for stress can vary greatly from person to person. Parents, for example, may become stressed by comparing their children to others and may end up yelling at them for not achieving what their neighbor's children have. However, it is important to remember that every child has unique qualities, Sanskar and interests, and it is unfair to compare them with others.

- Students get stressed because of exam fear.

- Manager gets stressed because of target completion.
- Employee gets stressed because of performance pressure.
- A woman gets stressed because her friend bought a new branded purse.
- Someone gets stressed because of an empty wallet.

The above is the reason for Stress. You all will be agreeing to this. But think again, whether we should be stressed due to the reasons listed above?

- Students don't study and blame the examiner for his stress.
- The manager did not put resources and money into achieving his target and blamed his boss for his stress.
- Employee did not put all his efforts, did not utilize his resources properly, and blamed his manager for his stress.

If these are not treated on time, it may lead to anxiety, fear, insecurity, irritation, anger, etc. The reason for this, I find is Comfort Zone. We fail to respond to the problems in the correct way, which is the reason for stress. The moment we change our perspective and think of a problem or situation like a play or movie or someone else problem, we won't feel stressed. During the pandemic, we used to do self-care. Here it is also the same; we need to care for ourselves. Attention on Me is called Mediatation.

Meditation= Me + Attention

Stress is not caused by more working hours, but rather by the state of mind towards a situation.

Do you think, if the same task is given to two people, they will respond the same way? One may feel stressed while doing it, and the other may do it happily. Why is it so? It is mainly due to his capacity, knowledge, and self-resilience (inner power). The other person who is stressed has to change his perspective and has to think that if the other person can do it happily, I should also do it with the same spirit and challenge.

Another reason for stress is our tendency to stick to old habits and routines. However, if we don't make any changes to our approach, we will keep getting the same outcomes. Only by trying something new and altering our habits can we expect to see different results.

How To Manage Stress

1. **Be Light:**

   Those who have a subtle intellect will be able to mould themselves according to circumstance. They will have the courage to confront anything. They will never be confused, but they will go into the depths of whatever the situation is and move according to that. Only when you are light will you be able to mould yourselves. When attempting to mold something, it must first be warm and soft. Without both of these qualities, it cannot be shaped. The object is heated until it becomes soft enough to be molded. What is the warmth and softness here? The softness is humility, and the warmth is the form of power. Humility means the form of love. Those who have a love for every soul will be able to remain humble. If there is no love, neither will they be able to become merciful nor will they be humble. This is why there has to be humility and the form of power. That is, to the extent that you are humble, there should be the feeling of being a master. There should be the feeling of being a master in the form of power; and in humility, there should be the virtue of serving. There should be service and also the feeling of being a master. When you have both this softness and warmth, you will be able to mould yourself in every aspect.

   You will remain light in all aspects. They remain light in their thoughts, light in their speech, light in their actions, and light in their relationships. If there is lightness in these four aspects, then that is the stage of an angel. So now, check: To what extent is there lightness in these four aspects? Those who are light will be able to recognize the sanskaras of any soul within a second. And they will also be able to decide, within a second, about whatever circumstance comes in front of them.

2. **Increase inner Power:**

   As I mentioned earlier, the problem persisted even during the pandemic. However, we have been using masks to protect ourselves and boost our immunity to fight against it. We are determined to find a solution and not let the problem persist any longer. First and foremost, it's important to boost our immunity and increase our inner strength. Problems can seem overwhelming, like mountains that are impossible to move. However, when we have a strong sense of inner power, those problems become more manageable. In fact, they may even seem like small seeds that can grow into something positive, like cotton. To increase our inner power, practicing Raj Yoga Meditation can be a helpful tool. A project manager should always keep themselves updated with their knowledge and revise the tools they have. This is like a soldier going to war without his weapons; without the proper tools, the project manager will not be able to handle thc situation efficiently. It is important to use the right tool for the right situation. When we feel cold, we wear warm clothes instead of blaming winter. Similarly, to be successful as a project manager, one needs to rewire their brain and focus on using the right tools for each situation.

   Man has conquered space & the elements. But he has not yet conquered his inner space.

3. **Be a Detached observer.**

   What is a detached observer? A detached observer is one involved in the activity physically and mentally but not emotionally. He will not be affected or influenced by the outcome. He will be enjoying the scene as a spectator sitting in the stadium or as a player in the game. It doesn't mean that you are not taking care of your work or people. The best example is a Nurse. The nurse is working in the hospital with complete dedication. She takes care of the child in the hospital during his duty hours, and her mind is always in the house, thinking of her own child.

As a detached observer, you won't be affected by the external environment. For instance, an essence stick (Agarbatti) is not affected by any bad smells in the air. Instead, it changes the environment. You, too, are a powerful soul. So, spread your positive vibrations - they will suppress any external unpleasant odors.

Challenges can be approached like a game by someone who is detached.

4. **Remove waste thoughts:**

   There was a monkey who was jumping from one branch of a tree to another. Unfortunately, he got a cut on his leg. He instinctively touched his skin to assess the damage, and in doing so, he opened the gap further to see how big the cut was. Another monkey noticed what had happened and came over to inspect the wound. He too opened the gap of the cut to see how big it was. This process continued with other monkeys who saw what was happening and came over to inspect the wound.

   Similarly, when we face a problem, we tend to create multiple thoughts about it, analysing and over-analysing the situation.

   How did this situation come to me?

   What will I do now?

   It is always coming to me.

   I would have done this if it had come my way.

   It is because of him.

   Also, whenever we meet another person, we will describe the same things to each and every person. This way we are giving power to the problem. Whereas we should not discuss too much with others. If we discuss it, it means we remember the problem and feel more stressed. Don't discuss negative thoughts. Increase positive thoughts.

5. **Thought and action are not aligned.**

   Sometimes, it has been observed that our thoughts, actions, and words are not perfect situations, and later on, you feel that I should have done like this. You repent of your decision. What will you call this?

   "Speak less, Speak sweetly, Speak slowly."

   You might have seen someone who speaks more, but you will find he doesn't have control over his speaking. Consider- My words have power. I speak the truth, I don't fear.

   If you think before you act, then you gainfully. You should not just check yourselves at night and in the morning, but also check yourselves before doing anything. Only then you do whatever you have to. It is just as important as when some people (Big people) first have to have their food inspected before they eat it.

6. **Treat it as a Test Paper**

   If you are in the examination hall, a question paper comes to you. What do you do? At that moment, a good student will be ready to answer. He will go through the questions and start answering them one by one with his best knowledge, and he will pass the exam. A Project is also the same. One should not question, why this situation came to my project. I haven't studied about this. You should not panic. You should analyse the problem and ask questions to yourself or to your team. Start with 'Why, What, Where, how' to find out the best possible solution but not blame anyone. Apply the best possible efforts to resolve, and you will succeed. There is always an option B for your problem.

7. **Power to Face**

   If you have any desire, you can not face it. Kaamana ki to Saamna nahi kar sakte.

8. **Don't cry to Release Stress**

   Crying is supported as a stress buster. I would say you should not cry; Human is the most powerful creation in this universe. He has the capability to fight with the situation.

   For the period you are crying, you are in a state of negative emotions. Probably you may feel like stress is reduced. But the cause of stress is still there. One should not waste time crying and seeking the attention of anyone else. He should be thinking about the solutions.

   Sometimes, people may face a hard time in their lives when they cry. That is okay, but this situation rarely comes where he can't find any solution; he feels disheartened. I would suggest that everyone should have someone in his life who gives support and strength and motivates him to bounce back.

   If a person makes the habit of crying, it may lead to depression, which is to be avoided for sure.

9. **Avoid temporary solution**

   Many of us believe that engaging in activities such as watching movies, shopping, smoking, drinking, or going on vacation will help to reduce our stress. However, we often find that as soon as the activity is over and we return to our normal routine, the stress returns. While these distractions may provide temporary relief, they do not address the root cause of the stress and do not provide a long-term solution to eliminate it from our lives.

   It's like a mother telling her son to watch cartoons on TV to distract him from the pain of his broken leg. Is it a solution?

10. **Sit with yourself**

Spend some time with yourself without doing anything, in solitude. Practice this every day, and you will get the solution from your subconscious mind.

Exercise:

Sit in a place where you feel calm and silent. You detached yourself from the outer world. Close your eyes. You sit on the floor in a yoga pose. Take a deep breath.....

You inhale and exhale, and you observe the breath is coming and going from one nostril to another...You concentrate on your nostril for some time...

Now, take your consciousness towards your head, you feel what is happening over there, what is the sensation there, then you come to your forehead, then both eyes, nose, mouth, and neck, and you try to observe what sensation is there. Then you move to the right hand, shoulder, elbow, wrist, palm, and finders, the same way to the left hand, your chest, stomach, back, lower back, right leg, thigh, knee, calf, ankle, and fingers, then the same way take your conscious to the left leg.

Now you in reverse order from leg to head. This one cycle will take about 10-15 minutes. You can repeat this cycle at least two times.

Now, you take your conscience inside you. Who am I? What is my purpose in this life? Am I doing the things that I am supposed to do? God has sent me for a special purpose. He wants me to do something special for the world. Give thought to yourself. I am achieving all the success in my life; I am achieving all my set targets, and I extend my gratitude to my family, friends, my teachers... thank you.....thank you.....I thank this nature who is giving me food, water, and shelter....I thank everyone.

I beg pardon to whom I have done wrong with them. I am sorry......Please forgive me......I have done it inadvertently. Now I realize my mistakes...please forgive me.... I am sorry. Now you can feel that they are forging me......They are saying to me, it is ok....I forgive you....In response, I say thank you for your kindness.....thanks a lot...

I am visualizing those people in front of me...those who have done wrong to me...., who betrayed me....., who cheated me......who did not cooperate in my time of need....I forgive everyone....I forgive everyone......I forgive everyone. They are free now. They are all my good friends. We all are enjoying our life happily. Life is so beautiful. Thank you, life, Thank you, God. Thank you, Nature; thank you, universe.

I am a powerful soul.

I have complete confidence in myself.

I am completing my tasks on time.

I am enjoying my work.

I have a good relationship with my family and my boss.

Everyone is supporting me.

I am enjoying this life, such a wonderful life I have.

Everyone likes me, loves me.

I have enough money.

I am very healthy.

My body organs are perfectly fine. Thanks to my body organs.

Again, I put my attention to my breath. I observe the breath is coming and going. And open your eyes slowly......You feel relaxed and energized. We need to do this exercise every morning and evening for about 30 minutes. It is good to do this practice early in the morning at 4:00 AM, This time is called Brahma Muhurta, Nectar time. The time when there is no traffic between you and the universe, You can manifest whatever you want.

I would suggest that one should practice this for a month,

if he feels that he is not getting any advantage, then he can stop. But I can guarantee he will find the magic within himself in less than a month.

11. **Learn new skills**

    In the event that you do what you are continuously doing, you will get what you have consistently got. When you learn new skills, you get the motivation to do work in a smarter way and accept the challenges. Your performance increases. Chances to blame others are reduced. You create positive thoughts. You will not be wasting time. You will be keeping yourself busy while learning. People don't want to change themselves, so you need to target 1% of the change in your life, and slowly, you can build new habits. Take baby steps to develop changes.

12. **Acceptance**

    Whatever is happening around you, you need to accept. Don't ask any questions that

    - Why is it happening?
    - It should not be happening this way.
    - Who is responsible for this?
    - How can you do like this?

    Whatever is happening, I have nothing to do with it. I will not get disturbed. I will remain calm and silent.

13. **Feel yourself as a Trustee**

    What does a trustee do? A trustee manages the property or assets of a person. He doesn't owe the ownership of the property. He is not emotionally attached to it. He takes care of the property without fear. If there is fear, there will be stress. You will not feel attached to it. This way, we can keep our minds calm, relaxed, and at ease. One who is simple is the one who is free from pain.

    We spend our whole life gaining assets and, after that, holding them and stressed of thing about losing them.

14. **Avoid Negative Content**

How should we start our day? The first thing we get up in the morning, do we want to read news papers immediately? Or open the news channel first?

If we are doing so, what are we consuming early in the morning? All Negative things because of what comes in the headlines of the news papers. It always starts with negative news. The same is happening in the news channels.

If we keep on consuming such kind of negative things, then we are definitely depleting our energy. We should be charging ourselves with positive thoughts and energy by consuming higher vibrational things such as prayer, reading spiritual and motivational books, meditation, etc.

15. **Keep Yourself Busy**

If you have free time, you may have unproductive thoughts. To stay focused and powerful, keep yourself busy and create a schedule for yourself. Just like you make a schedule for your physical activities, make one for your mental activities too. Plan to keep your mind busy so that you can continuously progress.

16. **Be Contented**

This is very complicated and difficult to understand the meaning of Contented. If you are contented with your desire or if you are satisfied with what you have, then you cant grow in your life.

Being content does not entail taking it easy and never experiencing additional success. Instead of living in continual fear and the need for more and more, satisfaction is the ability to remain content while achieving success.

17. **Forgive and Forget**

Whatever has been done in the whole day. If someone hurt you or insulted you, you forgive him and you have done something wrong to someone, then you need to beg pardon from him. This activity is to be done before you hit the bed and every day.

There may be other methods as well to reduce stress, which are not listed here. You can find your methods as well.

The myth is Managing Stress is difficult.

Interviewer: We heard a lot from you. You have gathered good knowledge from your father. I can't stop myself from meeting your father. The Father creates a nest for children, just as birds create a nest for their little ones. Can I meet him?

Son: He could not come due to his commitment to other important things. But his teaching is always with me.

Interviewer: Don't you feel upset as your father is not with you today on such a wonderful occasion?

Son: No. I don't. If he was here, he would have reminded me "Not to get attached to your success. One should not be affected by his success or failure. He needs to move on for his next achievement."

Inspirational Quotes

1. I wake up early because I need to wake the sun up. – Author
2. The best teacher is one who teaches himself to elevate his stage.
3. Do not plead your case but be your own judge.
4. Change your own attitude instead of taking revenge.
5. Desiring the rewards of your acts is like eating unripe fruit.
6. One thorn of weakness can ruin a whole bouquet of virtues.
7. First think and then act; in this way, you save time and energy.
8. Enthusiasm and alertness contribute greatly to your success.
9. Success is Key to determination.
10. Forgive and be forgiven.
11. Pure thoughts are your precious treasures.
12. Speak honestly but sweetly.
13. Create solution, end problem.
14. Keep Thought, Word & Deed in Harmony.
15. Fill your attitude with goodness.
16. Your every action is creating destiny.
17. Nor ordinary but be Extraordinary.
18. Keep your mind calm and body active.
19. Be open to positive change.
20. Value every lesson of life.
21. Deserve before you desire.
22. The one who has cleanliness within wins the hearts of others.

23. Cooperation comes when there are pure feelings and good wishes for all involved in the task.
24. Habits break easily when there is flexibility.
25. When there is the faith that things will turn out to be the best, there is enjoyment is whatever life brings.
26. When there is faith, there is happiness visible in my every thought, word and action.
27. Determination can change even opportunities and make things happen right.
28. True determination is a combination of single-mindedness and flexibility.
29. The gem cannot be polished without friction, nor man perfected without trials.
30. Deeds are like seeds; they take their own time to fructify.
31. The difference between the impossible and the possible lies in a person's determination.
32. If you want to live a happy life, tie it to a goal, not to people or things. - Albert Einstein
33. If you are depressed, you are living in the past. If you are anxious you are living in the future. If you are at peace you are living in the present. - Lao Tzu
34. The activity you're most avoiding contains your biggest opportunity. - Robin S. Sharma
35. Today i will do what others won't so tomorrow i can do what others can't. - Jerry Rice
36. Turn your face to the sun and the shadows fall behind you. - Maori Proverb
37. Do it now, don't leave for tomorrow or day after.
38. Determination is the key to success.
39. Life is a rollercoaster ride, full of ups and downs. Enjoy the ride.
40. "All of us do not have equal talent, but all of us have

an equal opportunity to develop our talents." -A. P.J. Abdul Kalam

41. Life is a project, need to manage properly.
42. Yesterday is history, tomorrow is mystery. Today is the gift. That's why it is called the Present. - Eleanor Roosevelt.
43. A man who dares to waste one hours of life has not discovered the value of life- Charles Darwin
44. Live each day as if it is your last day. – Marcus Aurelius
45. Don't say you don't have enough time. You have exactly the same number of hours per day that wear given to Hellen Keller, Pasteur, Michelangelo, Mother Teresa, Leonardo da Vinci, Thomas Jeffeson and Albert Einstein. – H. Jackson Brown.
46. A wise person does at once what a fool does at last. Both do the same thing, only at different times. - Baltasar Gracian
47. Better three hours too soon than one minute too late. - William Shakespeare
48. Don't be fooled by the calendar. There are only as many days in a year as you make use of. One man gets only a week's value out of the year, while another man gets a full year's value out of the week. – Charles Richards
49. Even if you are on the right track, you will get run over, if you just sit there. – Will Rogers
50. I made this letter longer than usual because I lack the time to make it shorter. – Pascal
51. He that rises late must trot all day. – Benjamin Franklin
52. He who gains time gains everything. – Benjamin Disraeli

53. I recommend to you to take care of minutes; hours will take care of themselves. – Lord Chesterfield
54. Life begins at the end of your comfort zone." - Neale Donald Walsch.
55. It is better to have lived one day as a tiger than a thousand years as a sheep. – Tibetan saying
56. It is better to do the right thing slowly than the wrong thing quickly. – Peter Turla
57. It's not enough to be busy, so are the ants. The question is, what are we busy about. – henry David Thoreau
58. Lost time is never found again. – Proverb
59. Never leave till tomorrow which you can do today. – Benjamin Franklin
60. Lost wealth may be replaced by industry, lost knowledge by study, lost health by temperance or medicine, but lost time is gone forever. – Samuel Smiles
61. Many people take no care of their money till they come nearly to the end of it, and others do just the same with their time. – Goethe
62. Money, I can only gain or lose. But time I can only lose. So I must spend it carefully. – Unknown
63. Nothing is ours except time. – Goethe
64. Ordinary people think merely of spending time. Great people think of using it. Unknown
65. Realize that in this moment of time, you are creating your next moment. – Sara Paddison
66. The surest way to be late is to have plenty of time. – Leo Kennedy
67. Those who make the worst use of their time are the first to complain of its shortness. – Jean De La Bruyere

68. Time is a greater healer but a poor beautician. – Lucille Harper
69. Time is money. – Benjamin Franklin
70. Time is a school in which you learn, time is a fire in which you burn. – Delmore Schwartz
71. Time stays long enough for those who use it. – Leonardo Da Vinci
72. Time will take your money, but money won't buy time, - James Taylor
73. If people are not laughing at your goals, your goals are too small. - Azim Premji
74. Great minds discuss ideas. Average minds discuss events. Small minds discuss people. - Eleanor Roosevelt
75. An entire sea of water can't sink a ship unless it gets inside the ship. Similarly, the negativity of the world can't put you down unless you allow it to get inside you. - Goi Nasu
76. It does not matter how slowly you go as long as you do not stop. - Confucius
77. Life has no remote. Get up and change it yourself." – Mark A. Cooper
78. Stay away from negative people. They have a problem for every solution." – Albert Einstein
79. Using someone else's ruler to measure your self-worth will always leave you short. - Charles F. Glassman
80. There is only one boss: the customer. And he can fire everybody in the company, from the chairman on down, simply by spending his money somewhere else. --Sam Walton
81. The minute you start caring about what other people think, is the minute you stop being yourself. --Meryl Streep

82. The bad news is time flies. The good news is you're the pilot. - Michael Altshuler

83. Keep your face always toward the sunshine, and shadows will fall behind you. — Walt Whitman

1. AUTHOR'S NEXT RELEASE

1. PS: BOOK COVER, TITLE OR SUBTITLE MAY CHANGE BEFORE PUBLISHING